ISBN 978-1-4950-0889-4

HAL•LEONARD®
CORPORATION
7777 W. BLUEMOUND RD. P.O. BOX 13819 MILWAUKEE, WI 53213

For all works contained herein:
Unauthorized copying, arranging, adapting, recording, Internet posting, public performance,
or other distribution of the printed music in this publication is an infringement of copyright.
Infringers are liable under the law.

LIVE LIFE

Words and Music by JESSE UECKE,
JOY UECKE, NATE CAMPANY
and ALLAN GRIGG

© 2014 WARNER CHAPPELL MUSIC MEXICO S.A. DE C.V., DEAR CLEVELAND PUBLISHING, WHERE DA KASZ AT?, KOJAKTRAX and PRESCRIPTION SONGS
All Rights in the U.S. and Canada for WARNER CHAPPELL MUSIC MEXICO S.A. DE D.V. Administered by WB MUSIC CORP.
All Rights for DEAR CLEVELAND PUBLISHING and WHERE DA KASZ AT? Administered Worldwide by SONGS OF KOBALT MUSIC PUBLISHING
All Rights for KOJAKTRAX and PRESCRIPTION SONGS Administered Worldwide by KOBALT SONGS MUSIC PUBLISHING
All Rights Reserved   Used by Permission

THE APOLOGY SONG

Lyric by PAUL WILLIAMS
Music by GUSTAVO SANTAOLALLA

Copyright @ 2014 T C F Music Publishing, Inc. and Sunset Squid Music
All Rights Reserved   Used by Permission

NO MATTER WHERE YOU ARE

Words and Music by
MICHAEL ALVARADO

Moderately fast

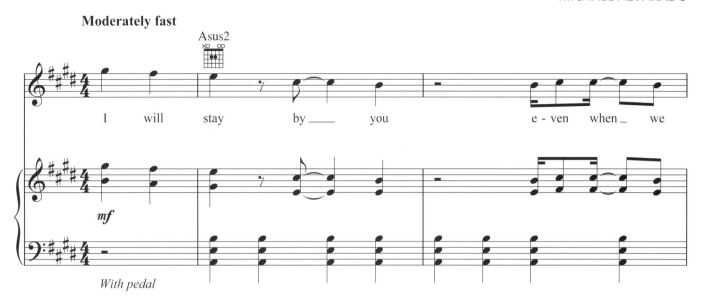

I will stay by ___ you e - ven when ___ we

fall. I will be the rock ___ that holds you up ___ and

lifts you high ___ so you can stand tall. I won't

Copyright © 2014 Sony/ATV Music Publishing LLC and Michael Alvarado Music
All Rights Administered by Sony/ATV Music Publishing LLC, 424 Church Street, Suite 1200, Nashville, TN 37219
International Copyright Secured   All Rights Reserved

I LOVE YOU TOO MUCH

Words and Music by PAUL WILLIAMS
and GUSTAVO SANTAOLALLA

Copyright © 2014 TCF Music Publishing, Inc. and Sunset Squid Music
All Rights Reserved   Used by Permission

I WILL WAIT

Words and Music by
MUMFORD & SONS

Bright Polka

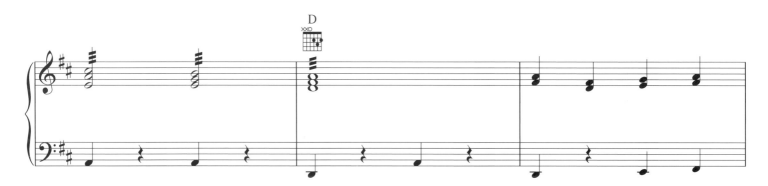

Copyright © 2012 UNIVERSAL MUSIC PUBLISHING LTD.
All Rights in the U.S. and Canada Controlled and Administered by UNIVERSAL - POLYGRAM INTERNATIONAL TUNES, INC.
All Rights Reserved   Used by Permission

Children: I'll be bold _____ as

THE ECSTASY OF GOLD

By ENNIO MORRICONE

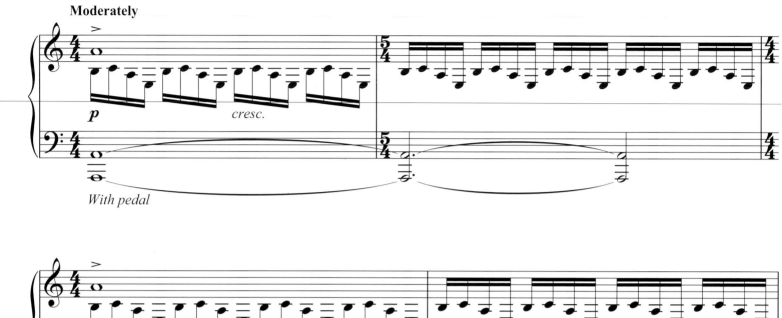

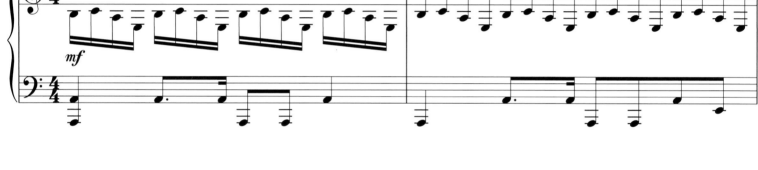

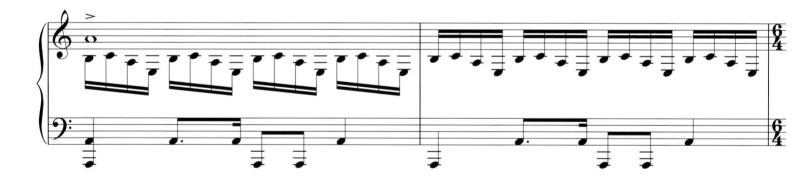

© 1966, 1968 (Copyrights Renewed) EDIZIONI EUREKA (Italy)
All Rights in the U.S. and Canada Administered by EMI UNART CATALOG INC.
Exclusive Print Rights Controlled and Administered by ALFRED MUSIC
All Rights Reserved   Used by Permission

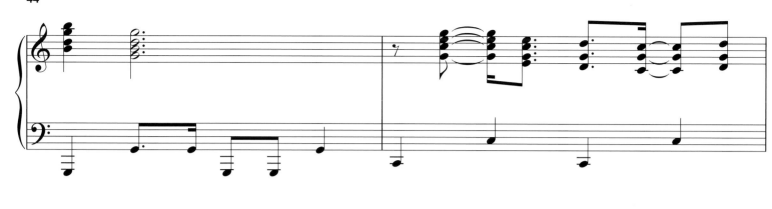

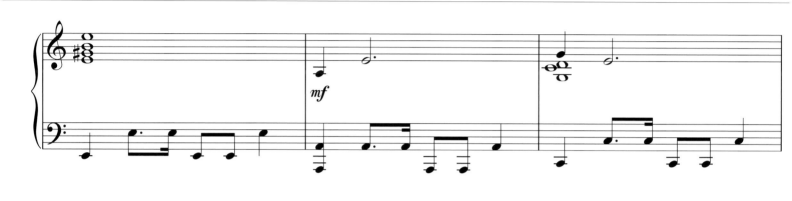